LITTLE BIG BOOK PLUS

Table of Contents

Meet
Shari Halpern

Shari Halpern wrote *My River* when she was in art school. To get writing and drawing ideas, she visited the nearby Hudson River.

Shari Halpern, Age 7

"The river belongs to everyone, so I made that the theme of my book," says Ms. Halpern.

MY RIVER

by Shari Halpern

HOUGHTON MIFFLIN COMPANY

BOSTON

ATLANTA   DALLAS   GENEVA, ILLINOIS   PALO ALTO   PRINCETON

For their help with this book, I would like to thank John Cronin, Alan Reingold, Judy Sue Goodwin-Sturges, Beverly Reingold, Jean Krulis, James P. Rod, and Lynne O'Malley.

Acknowledgments

Text

For each of the selections listed below, grateful acknowledgment is made for permission to excerpt and/or reprint original or copyrighted material, as follows:

1 *My River,* written and illustrated by Shari Halpern. Copyright © 1992 by Shari Halpern. Reprinted by permission of Macmillan Books for Young Readers, Simon & Schuster Children's Publishing Division.

Photography

i Tony Scarpetta. **ii** Courtesy of Shari Halpern. **33** Bequest of William Sturgis Bigelow. Courtesy, The Museum of Fine Arts, Boston. **34** ZEFA/The Stock Market (l); N.Y. Gold/ZEFA/The Stock Market (tr); © John Warden/Tony Stone Images Inc. (br). **35** ZEFA/The Stock Market (t); © 1994 Animals Animals/James D. Watt (bl); © Animals Animals/Richard Shiell (br). **36** © Willard Clay/Tony Stone Images, Inc. (t); © 1992 Ivan Massar/Positive Images (b). **37** Tony Scarpetta (tr, bl, br); Tracey Wheeler (c). **38** Tony Scarpetta (r); Tracey Wheeler (tl, cl, bl).

1999 Impression

Houghton Mifflin Edition, 1996
Copyright © 1996 by Houghton Mifflin Company. All rights reserved.

Printed in the U.S.A.

ISBN 0-395-73155-0

14 15 - B - 98

For Maw, Pop, and Maura,
who are pleased and proud

and for Jaclyn,
who would have been

Whose river is this?

It's my river.

It's our river.

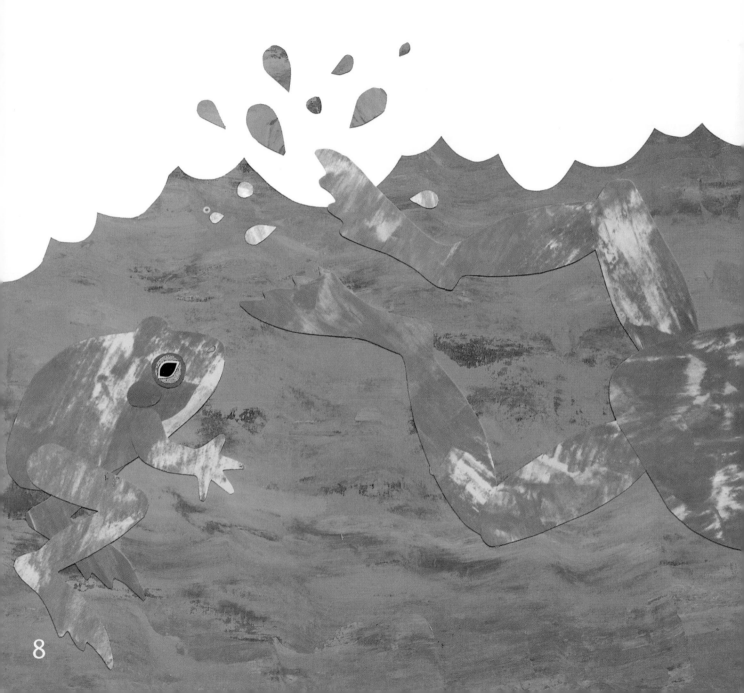

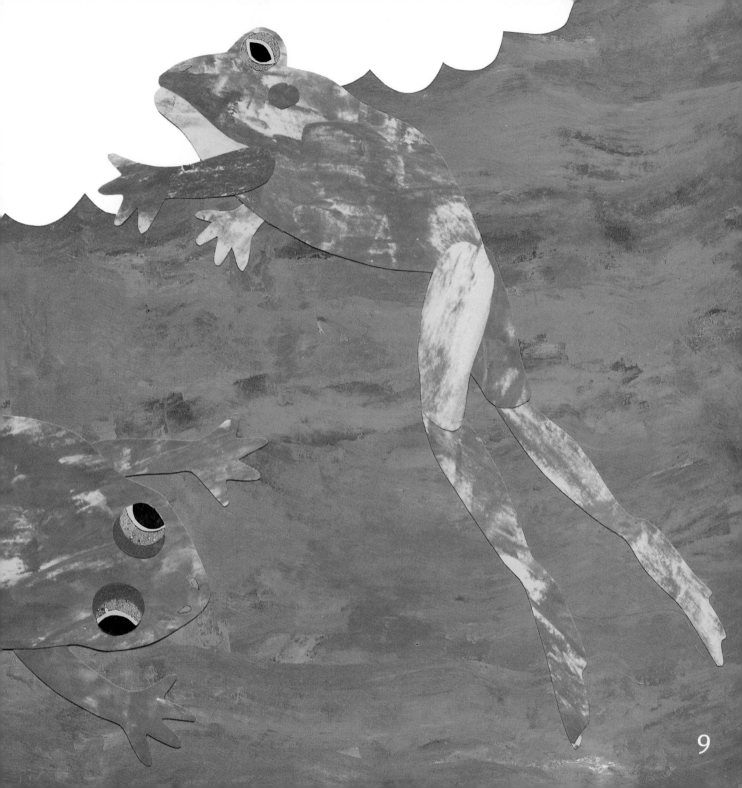

9

It's everyone's river!

This is my home.

We live here, too.

16

I was born here.

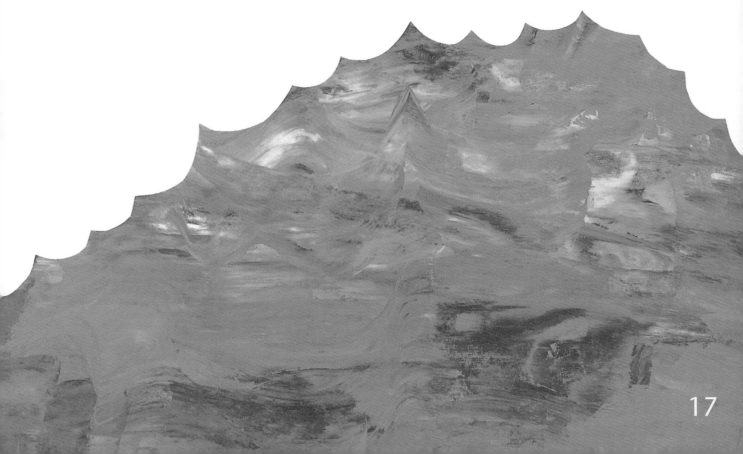

This is where we grow.

19

I need the river.

So do we.

24

We *all* need the river!

This river is mine.

27

Whose river is it?

It's *everyone's* river!

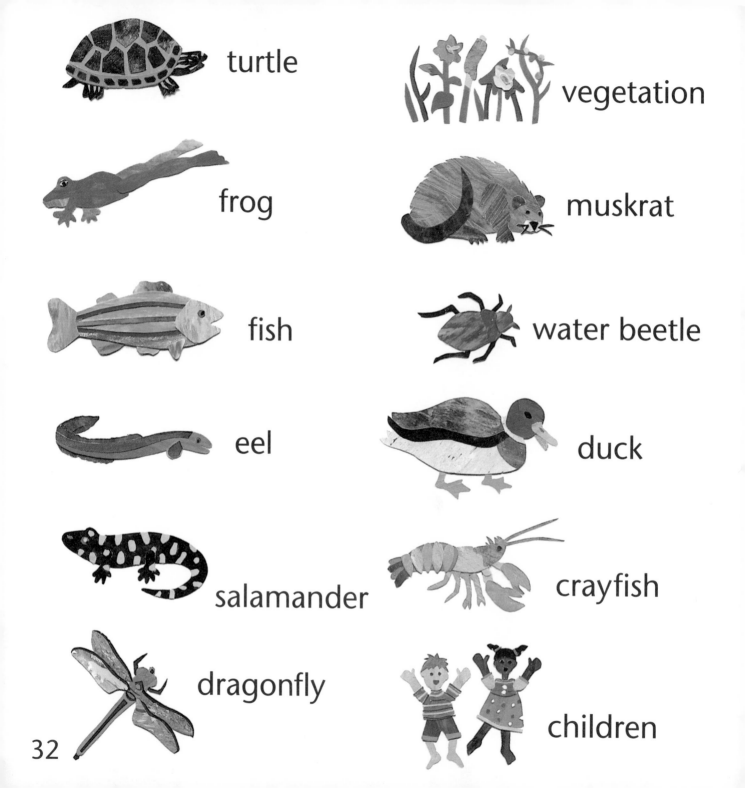

turtle

vegetation

frog

muskrat

fish

water beetle

eel

duck

salamander

crayfish

dragonfly

children

32

The Blue Boat
by Winslow Homer

Winslow Homer loved to spend time outdoors.
He painted what he saw and liked best. Look at
this watercolor painting and tell what he saw.

River Life

Pelicans
Ewaso Ng'Iro River, Kenya

Elephant
Zambezi River,
Zimbabwe

Bear
Toklat River, Alaska

Hippopotamuses
Victoria Nile, Uganda

Dragonfly
**Santa Clara River,
California**

Manatee
Homosassa River, Florida

Reeds
Rio Grande River,
New Mexico

Lupine
Merrimack River,
Massachusetts

Whose River Is This?

What do you think happened
to this river?

It's Everybody's River!

What are these people doing?
What could you do to help a river?